Louise Clarkson Whitelock

The Gathering Of The Lilies

Louise Clarkson Whitelock

The Gathering Of The Lilies

ISBN/EAN: 9783337149772

Printed in Europe, USA, Canada, Australia, Japan

Cover: Foto ©Andreas Hilbeck / pixelio.de

More available books at **www.hansebooks.com**

The

Gathering of the Lilies.

Illustrated by the author,

L. (CLARKSON) Whitelock

AUTHOR OF

"Violet, with Eyes of Blue."

Colored Plates and Lithographic Etching.

PHILADELPHIA

J. L. SIBOLE & CO.

PUBLISHERS.

JANSEN. McCLURG & CO., CHICAGO.

A. HOEN & CO.

Lithographers and Printers, Baltimore, Md.

Table of Contents.

Poems.

Illustrations.

DEDICATED

TO F. S.

___

REMEMBRANCE.

"For the calm thy kindness lent
To a path of discontent,
Rough with trial and dissent;

Gentle words where such were few,
Softening blame where blame was true,
Praising where small praise was due;

For a waking dream made good,
For an ideal understood,
For thy christian womanhood;

For thy marvelous gift to cull
From our common life and dull
Whatsoe'er is beautiful;

Thoughts and fancies, Hybla's bees
Dropping sweetness; true heart's-ease
Of congenial sympathies;—

Still for these I own my debt;
Memory with her eyelids wet,
Fain would thank thee even yet!

And as one who scatters flowers
Where the Queen of May's sweet hours
Sits, o'ertwined with blossomed bowers,

In superfluous zeal bestowing
Gifts where gifts are overflowing,
So I pay the debt I'm owing,

Well assured that thou wilt take
Even the offering which I make
Kindly for the giver's sake."

J. G. Whittier.

The Gathering of the Lilies.

Japan Lily.

W are lilies, every one
Nodding brightly to the sun,
Proud and happy to be won
        By his glance.
Not a flower is so gay
As we are, the live-long day,
And with butterflies we play
        And flit and dance."

Garden Lily.

W are royal lilies, too,

Just as richly born as you,

And we bear the perfume true

In our breath.

But in quiet we would grow,

In the zephyr swinging slow:

We think life is easier so,

And easier death."

l

Meadow Lily.

'm a tiny Meadow Lily;

You great flowers call me silly

And you look so very chilly

When you smile.

But the children love to play

With me every Summer day:

If you've children here, I'll stay

Just a while.

I

Lily of the Valley.

Pass us by, for we are pale,

Little lilies of the vale;

God hath made us very frail,

    Yet we give

Love to all the flowers that grow,

And the flowers love us so;

We are happier than you know,

    Just to live.

Day Lily.

W are lilies, looking down,
Modest in our glistening gown
As the cow-slip dressed in brown;
    For we say,
Surely we are born in state;
But our honors will not wait,
And our life, early and late,
    Is a day.

Tiger Lily

"Surely, friends, I bear your name;
Do not look at me with blame,
And so sadly put to shame
　　My yellow face.

I am lily-born like you;
But the morning bath in dew
Will not make me fair to view
　　As my race."

W are lilies of the lake,

Never more than half awake;

Even in our dreams, we make

Music sweet.

We go sailing, sailing by,

Underneath the happy sky,

Happy at our ease to lie

In rest complete."

See where comes their lovely queen!

Down her robe of velvet green

Flows the royal satin sheen,

    Pearly white.

And her face is high and fair;

Never mortal queen could wear

Such a grand and stately air

    As this sprite.

To their sovereign low they bow;

Yet each would be first,—and now

Clamors each to deck her brow

    With honors sought.

But the valley-lily, from

The dark curtains of her home,

In her sweet content is dumb,

    Asking nought.

|

Callo Lily.

isten to th' imperious call:

　"Lilies! Lilies! silence all:

In my peerless presence fall

　　At my feet.

I have come my crown to share:—

On my bosom I will bear

The valley-lily, who is fair

　　As she is sweet."

To the Easter Lily.

.

To the Easter Lily.

O Easter Lily, lift your shining head;
　　Brush off the shadow of the barren mould;
For Winter, who hath bound you fast, is dead,
　　And Summer wooes you to his heart of gold.

Sleep, Christmas Lilies, 'neath the Christmas snow
　　For on your white lips is the kiss of death,
And while the happy hours come and go.
　　Still shall we wait and miss your fragrant breath.

Wake, O June Lilies! stir in your green beds,
　　Whisper life's secret to your listening heart;
The Sun, himself, shall crown your royal heads
　　When you have burst your thousand buds apart.

Bloom now, O Easter Lilies! wreathe and twine
　　Your silver stars around the glad, new earth;
The last year's leaf hath died that you may shine,
　　And there is Resurrection in your birth

April 1, 1877.

Fast Little Miss Crocus.

Fast Little Miss Crocus.

Time folks was gettin' up--
     They're so slow.
I've been awake here
     Hours ago!

Reckon I'll peep out:—
     Who's afraid?
That dark aint nothin',
     Only shade.

Been here long enough
     In my bed:
Guess I'll push blanket
     Off my head.

My Stars! what a world!
　　Ain't it white!
I b'lieve the clouds fell
　　Down in the night.

I smell somethin':
　　My! that's good!
Must be Arbutus
　　Up in the wood.

If there ain't Snow-drop!
　　Seems to me
She'd better stay where
　　She oughter be.

Wonder what brought her
　　Out so soon.
S'pose she thought 'twas
　　Afternoon.

She'll get her nose nipped:
　　Serve her right!
Small children like her
　　Must keep out o' sight.

Wind needn't blow so!
     Makes such a din.
Good gracious!—guess I'd
     Better go in.

Where's my blanket gone?
     Cold hurts so.
Poor little Crocus is
     Freezin' up—oh!

B'lieve I'm an orphan, now;
     —Goin' to—die!
And be—an angel—
     Up in the sky!

Buried Lilies.

BURIED LILIES.

WRITTEN FOR TAUBERT'S CRADLE SONG.

A white and wintry sky
 From which the snow-flakes fly:
A wide and white and wintry world.
To which the flying snow is hurled:
Whereon it lies, as we all must.
And, like us, mingles with the dust.
Where wait the flowers, in graves unseen.
 Until the Spring is green.

Across the plain, the sheep.
 Wet and forsaken creep:
The north-wind is not tempered to
The bleating lamb or shivering ewe.
Is there, nowhere, a sheltering fold
Where they can wait, from storm and cold,
For Summer shine, through Winter sheen.
 To make their pastures green?

A sad and hopeless heart,
    From which the tear-drops start,
And fall across the lonely life
Where joys are dead, and storms are rife;
Where skies have early lost their gold,
And far-off seems the sheltering fold:—
Yet hope has prayers, her tears between,
    And keeps her memory green.

O earth beneath thy snow!
    O heart beneath thy woe!
The snow melts lightly in the dust,
Through which the buried lilies thrust,
And grief and death shall pass away,
When God has brought us into day:
So through things seen, to the unseen,
    He keeps His Heaven green.

The Last Lily.

THE LAST LILY.

She seemed like one in a painful dream,
  And she brooded the whole day long:
And over and over she said to herself
  The words of the sad, lone song.

And in her lap, all wet with her tears,
  Was a lily, brown and dead—
"He kissed my hand when he gave me this;
  'Twas the last he gave me," she said.

And the anxious mother watched her face,
  And questioned her: "O Lucile,
Why will you dream this dream of woe,
  When you dreamed no dream of weal?

"You have said you would that he came no more;
  You have said he was nothing to you"—
"I was false to him in his life," she said,
  "In his death I will be true."

But the mother cried: "What is truth to him
  When it cometh now, too late?
What use to cherish a memory flower
  Beside the grave of his fate?

"He came and went through the Summer days,
  And you wished him far away;
You never longed for his coming then,
  Why long, my child, to-day?

"He came and went through the winter nights,
    And he vexed you—I know not how;
And you prayed, "forget me"—O Lucile!
    Why not forget him now?

"He came when the skies were fair or dark,
    And his presence was ever a cross"—
"O mother! How could I tell," she sobbed,
    That his absence would be loss?

"I might have loved him and blest his life
    That he kept so empty for me,"—
("Nay, dear, but his life," she said, "is filled
    With the things of eternity.")

"O hard remorse! why follow my soul
    With chidings all the day long?
He hath won more than love of mine could give
    And he hath forgotten the wrong."

"Nay, child, is it wrong when a woman's heart
    Cannot answer a good man's love?
If she's true, the angels will call her pure,
    And pity her, up above.

"O loss! O change! is it fair to throw
   Such a halo around his name,
When, if wishing were changed to reality,
   She must deny him the same?"

"O helpless retrospect! Why efface
   The truth, and leave but the dream?
If he could return, he would never be
   To her, what it makes him seem.

"If he came again from his radiant home,
   Where, at last, his love hath "forgot,"
With the old familiar look—Lucile,
   Would you welcome him back, or not?

"If you heard, to night, through the driving rain,
   The step you so often have heard,
I think you would turn away as before,
   And never give him a word.

"You would find, if his heart were just as warm,
   That yours could be just as cold,
And his wooing just as weary a thing,
   As ever in days of old."

"Stay, mother!" she cried—"in those careless years
    He was faithfulest, truest of men;
He loved me above all my waywardness,
    And I could not love him then;

"And I know, if his going home were a dream
    And I'd waken to find him to-day,
My woman's heart would be true to its fate,
    And I'd wish him far away.

"But because he hath grown unconscious of me,
    I would have him seek me yet;
And because I gave him not what he sought
    My life is sharp with regret.

"For he stretched out his arms to me to the end,
    And I helped him not. Now dim,
As his eyes in death, are mine with tears,
    And I stretch out my arms to him."

"You loved him not, yet you think of him so?
    Lucile, your words are wild;
His love was no more than other loves
    That are reaching to you, my child."

But she said: "Other loves are nothing to me,
    Because of one face I miss;
Because on my lap no lilies are laid,
    And on my hands no kiss.

"And his fond, fond love to my thought comes back,
    And I know it was pure and strong;
But I shall have it no more—no more,
    Tho' the years be ever so long.

"And I know, as the seasons come and go,
    And I sit here all alone,
I shall keep in my heart the old, sad song,
    And sing it for my own."

"How could I tell
* I would love him to-day,*
Whom that day I held not dear?
* How could I know*
* I would love him once,*
When I did not love him once?"

                  Jean Ingelow

Crowned.

CROWNED.

"As the lily among thorns, so is my love."

RABBONI! who hath crowned Thee with these thorns?
   O Master! who hath bowed Thy human head?
Who is it, Lord. that hath betrayed Thee thus?—
   '''Who is it?'—Thou, that speakest it, hast said'—
The careless one that dips with Me the bread.

"Ye deck Me in the purple of your scorn;
   The cross of your rejection is on Me;
And weeping angels see Me daily led,
   By your denials, unto Calvary:—
And ask ye, who can the betrayer be?"

O Jesus! and has He no human friends
   In all this weary cruel human place?
Will no one see the pathos of His love
   Upon His wounded, white, and stricken face,
And in the shameful thorns, His sufferings trace?

Oh! for some sinless, worthy, human hand
   To lift the marring thorns from off His brow.
O gentle King!—King of humility!
   No crown is half divine enough; for Thou
Art crowned with Thy majestic patience now.

"And would ye crown Me? O dim-sighted souls!
    Behold, My crown shall be your faithfulness.
Yet bring the meek white lilies, for a sign
    Among man's thorns, of God's forgivingness,
    And round my head the cool, wet petals press.

"Then shall I wear a crown so lowly, that
    The princes of this world deny my birth.
'I am the Lily of the Valleys,' and
    I scatter my white peace throughout the earth,
    And the redeemed, alone, confess its worth."

THE LILY OF ST. JOSEPH